speculative books

glasgow

all rights reserved

© copyright 2019

isbn: 978-1-912917-17-4

words by sean wai keung

www.speculativebooks.net

be happy
by sean wai keung

how to be authentic
this chinese new year

tiger woods

year of the pig

oj simpson

vespa

how to work
this city is too expensive

how can i help you

the hole

thoughts on commute

how to escape
the trap

things can only get better from here

whats the matter

be happy

how to communicate
the blooming

closer

the message

follow me

school prize

how to be authentic

this chinese new year

this chinese new year live in hope + warmth

this chinese new year be prosperous + happy

this chinese new year visit family + friends

this chinese new year dine out for only £10 as part of the new marks + spencer ultimate chinese feast meal deal featuring restaurant quality dishes such as sticky chinese pork ribs + chicken + mushroom in oyster + ginger sauce

this chinese new year look up your chinese zodiac animal but then forget again a few minutes later

this chinese new year ask your mixed-culture mixed-race friend what the chinese zodiac animals actually mean + when they say they dont know please dont say back to them how can you not understand your own culture

this chinese new year watch crouching tiger hidden dragon again

this chinese new year go pay respects to your ancestors

this chinese new year say *gun hei fat choi* to everyone even though you dont fully understand what *gun hei fat choi* really means or implies i mean its just happy new year right *gun-hei-fat-choi ha-ppy-new-year* – seems right this chinese new year start calling it lunar new year instead to show solidarity with all the other countries which also celebrate the same thing but arent called china

this chinese new year turn on the tv + watch ken hom cook chow mein + smile behind his dead cold eyes as he tries once again to sell you his woks

this chinese new year go to a chinese restaurant for a meal

this chinese new year look at the google homepage + check out their celebratory internet doodle

this chinese new year go into town + watch the dragon dancing + as a sign of extra respect film it all on your huawei phone before uploading it to twitter where it will get a handful of likes + one retweet

this chinese new year buy a drink for your east-asian diaspora friend + make sure they arent too stressed

this chinese new year remember your past but not too much

this chinese new year think about vincent chin who was literally killed by racists + who nobody seems to remember

this chinese new year dont think about that time you were the only eurasian kid in your class + you stupidly agreed to stand up in front of everyone + eat a bowl of rice in front of them in order to show how to eat chinese food authentically

this chinese new year eat rice but only in the authentic way

this chinese new year tell your family you love them even though you dont visit enough

this chinese new year remember the bradford race riots

this chinese new year buy a chinese new year inspired flower bouquet to send to your loved ones

this chinese new year open a fortune cookie after your meal

this chinese new year try once again to explain to your family your decision to try to become a creative instead of a lawyer or doctor or chef

this chinese new year turn to your fully white friends + ask them what they have done recently for their local east-asian diaspora community

this chinese new year do something nice for your local east-asian diaspora community

this chinese new year instead of regular chips eat chinese chips

this chinese new year book any and all good local east-asian diaspora artists for your creative events + openmics

this chinese new year hold your grandmothers hand + beg her once again to try to look after herself this chinese new year send around whatsapp videos of fatty chinese babies cutely saying *gun hei fat choi*

this chinese new year donate some money to charity

this chinese new year cook yourself a stir fry

this chinese new year dont be racist

this chinese new year eat more broccoli

this chinese new year believe in yourself more yes you have faults but at the same time all the good things you are putting out into the universe are recognised + worth it even if it doesnt seem that way

this chinese new year go to the zoo + watch pandas fail to fuck

this chinese new year tell your mother how you are worried you will never see your grandmother again since shes getting so frail now

this chinese new year clean your grandfathers grave + light incense for him even if theres a storm on

this chinese new year try not to cry as you say goodbye to them all

this chinese new year please be safe please be warm

this chinese new year go to an openmic + listen to someone do a chinese new year poem + please dont forget me if you dont see me again + please support as much local east-asian businesses as you can – even if all that means is buying a chinese new year takeaway munchy box

tiger woods

tiger woods is standing on my laptop smiling widely there is a commentator behind me + he says *this is a remarkable story*

tiger woods looks directly at me + asks if i would like to see his trophies

tiger woods asks me this while maintaining his same wide smile

i say to tiger woods that i have no interest in trophies

i say to tiger woods that i dont know anything about golf

i say to tiger woods that i need to use my laptop as i have many things to google

i say to tiger woods that while im happy that he is happy i myself am not

tiger woods does not get off my laptop nor does he stop smiling

he tells me that i should learn more about golf since it is such an interesting sport

he tells me that he has faced many problems in his life but he always knew he would make it back to the top

i say to tiger woods that while i am no expert on his life story i do seem to remember that those problems included extra-marital affairs + drink driving

tiger woods says yes those are my problems + then he asks me what mine are

i choose to ignore tiger woods question + instead i ask again for my laptop back

tiger woods says no + the commentator once again remarks

this is such a truly remarkable story

in 1997 tiger woods was being interviewed by oprah winfrey + she asked him if he thought of himself as an african-american

tiger woods responded by saying that when he was a kid he came up with the term cablinasian to describe himself – ca for caucasian – bl for black – in for indian – asian for asian

oprah winfrey replied by saying o thats what you call yourself

yeah said tiger woods

then they went to an ad break

i remind tiger woods of this story while he continues to stand on my laptop

i say that when i heard about it it made me want to

come up with my own term for myself
but that i realised that if you tried to combine ca for
caucasian with asian for asian
you just come up with caucasian again

tiger woods laughs at this + says i am a good kid
i ask him politely to not call me a kid but he just
continues to laugh

eventually he gets bored + says he needs to take a
leak + touch his trophies
he finally steps off from my laptop + disappears down
the hallway beyond my room
the commentator follows him closely
he says again *wow what a remarkable story*

i scramble over to my laptop + after wiping away the
footprints from where tiger woods stood i google 'tiger
woods'

after his official website + wikipedia page there are
several other articles about him
they include *Why Don't Women Get Comebacks Like
Tiger Woods*
+ *Tiger Woods Shows Up To His Restaurant Wearing
His Masters Green Jacket*

a few google pages along these articles start to get older along with *Tiger Woods Exposed As A Serial Cheater + Tiger Woods In DUI Scandal* there are others such as

Tiger Woods Once Again Denies His Blackness

just when im about to click on these articles tiger woods returns from his bathroom break + tells me to get off his laptop
he now has with him several trophies which the commentator is holding
remarkable the commentator whispers

i tell tiger woods that im sorry but i think that this particular laptop belongs to me

tiger woods looks confused but then breaks out again into his wide winners smile
he laughs + tells me again that im a good kid

i tell tiger woods that i think he may be a bad person trapped in a good person trapped in another bad person + so on
its like a russian doll type situation i say to him

tiger woods looks at his watch which is more valuable

than all of my possessions combined
i have to go play golf now he says

+ without so much as a goodbye he turns to leave
the commentator follows him as well
what a remarkable story the commentator says

+ then its just me again
alone in my room
with my laptop

year of the pig

she asks me what the year of the pig will mean for her
+ i say back *fuck if i know*
i dont mess with that astrology stuff
she asks why

i have prepared for this conversation already since it
always comes up
around lunar new year time – have practised answers
over + over
similar to what i do with other questions such as
where are you from or *what brings you here*
to which i always give one of a handful of premeditated
answers
depending on who is asking
for instance if they look genuinely curious i say
im half chinese half white + i came here because i had
to go somewhere
+ here seemed good

if they look more aggressive then its
im over on south side near queens park
+ i came here because i got offered a job

while for anyone between the two there are other

possible answers:

1. *one set of my grandparents are from hongkong while the others from england*
+ i came here to get away from them all
  [funny – will hopefully get a laugh – deflect]

2. *im from lots of places + i came here for a quiet drink*
  [short – bit abrasive – only use on those you know you could take]

3. *i studied in london for a bit then norwich which i hated*
but i knew that here would be better than those
  [for studenty types – easier to talk about education than origin]

4. mixed combination of the above
  [second part of answer may change depending on reaction to first part]

however perhaps because ive got a few drinks in me now
or maybe because i cant quite read
this girl or maybe because i find her attractive or i want her to find me attractive i forget

all my usually prepared answers to the astrology
question

i forget about the times i saw firsthand the stars used to
try to control behaviour
or the occasions my relationships were predicted to fail
+ then failed
the ages in my life declared unlucky ages which
truthfully turned out horrible
the memory of myself as a kid opening up
that big red book of star signs only to close it again at
the sight of my age of death

i could say any of those things + honestly i think they
would
be accepted
but instead all i can think to say is *i dont
like to know what my future holds*
which is a response with no predictable line
of reaction or conversation
no foreseeable follow up or end point
+ yet still she responds with a smile
fair enough she says with a shrug *me neither*

oj simpson

oj simpson is standing on my laptop smiling icily
there is a lawyer behind me + he says *this is not a race
issue*

oj simpson looks directly at me + asks if i would like to
see his heisman trophy
oj simpson asks me this while maintaining his same
wide smile
i say to oj simpson that i have no interest in trophies
i say to oj simspon that i dont know anything about
american football
i say to oj simpson that i need to use my laptop as i
have many things to google
i say to oj simpson that i know about his violent past

oj simpson does not get off my laptop nor does he stop
staring at me
he tells me that i should learn more about american
football since its such an interesting sport
he tells me that even when he was in prison he
coached the inmate football team

i say to oj simspon that i have watched many
documentaries about his life + i know he is a bad

person

oj simpson says he probably is but then asks me if i am too

i choose to ignore oj simpsons question + instead i ask again for my laptop back
oj simpson says no + the lawyer once again remarks
this is not a race issue

in 1995 at 10:07a.m oj simpson was acquitted on two counts of murder
an estimated 100 million people worldwide watched or listened to the verdict announcement
+ it was widely reported that the result was celebrated by majority black communities
while majority white communities were shocked + outraged

i remind oj simpson of this story while he continues to stand on my laptop
i say that when i saw the documentary footage on it i thought about what it would be like to have that many people watch you discover your fate

oj simpson laughs at this + says i am a good kid

i ask him politely to not call me a kid but he just continues to laugh

eventually he gets bored + says he needs to take a leak + touch his heisman
he finally steps off from my laptop + disappears down the hallway beyond my room
the lawyer follows him closely
he says again *this is not a race issue*

i scramble over to my laptop + after wiping away the footprints from where oj simpson stood i google

'oj simpson'

after his wikipedia page + official website there are several articles still about his murder case including *Five Things That Suggest O.J. Simpson Killed His Ex-Wife*

just when im about to click on this article oj simpson returns from his bathroom break + tells me to get off his laptop
he now has with him his heisman which the lawyer is holding
this is not a race issue the lawyer whispers

i tell oj simpson that im sorry but i think that this particular laptop belongs to me

oj simpson looks confused but then breaks out again into his sinister cold smile
he laughs + tells me again that im a good kid

i tell oj simpson that i dont think there is any good in him but that this doesnt mean i think he has always been bad

oj simpson looks at his watch which is more valuable than all of my possessions combined
i have to go now he says

+ without so much as a goodbye he turns to leave
the lawyer follows him as well
this really isnt a race issue the lawyer says

+ then its just me again
alone in my room
with my laptop

vesta

nothing like the real thing, it's a thing unto
itself... unsurpassed in its field,
dehydrated food at its curious best

– an amazon review of vesta chow mein
3-pack ready meals

thank you goddess of freeze dried meats
authentically colour schemed packaging
goddess of the home + hearth you provide
connection between worlds otherwise
separated by seas etc. but now together
again with thanks also to the powers
of microwaves + electricity we watch you
spin like a kid watches a marble in a marble
machine – without you we would not be here
without you who would supply our demands
within our economic/time-sensitive modern
lives without you how else would we fill
the gap between us all – our individual
servings of taste/belief + unwavering hunger

how to work

this city is too expensive

i should leave but where
would i go its not like
theres anywhere out there
right for me at least thats
what the where-should-you-live quiz said
on my laptop which is always on + next
to my bed which i am always in

      - this is no place for those who want
      to reset + dont you want to be famous
      for being where you belong but you cant
      you will always be remembered here if not
      for your smile then for the tiny imprints
      you leave branded
      on that pillow you have always been
      too poor to hold onto

the hole

wake to dripping realise
there is a hole in my room
by the window

the storm outside makes this hole
seem necessarily epic at this time
of the morning

[related:]

make a coffee + calm down
send positive thoughts out to the hole - you will
not break today - you are only a hole

[unrelated:]

remember being told my coffee tastes
like weetabix remember an unrelated incident
where i was force-fed weetabix
it tasted like shit

[related:]

i cant believe i have to work today

i havent had a day off in so long
sunday doesnt count as i had to do things
washing shopping replying to emails
that isnt any kind of day off

[unrelated:]

the only reason i am noticing this hole
is because of the storm outside - once the storm
finishes i will go back to not noticing it at all

[related:]

but it will still be there

[unrelated:]

coffee is half-finished if i drink any more i will die
cant believe i have to work today
cant believe i need an umbrella but dont have one
cant believe i will never eat cereal again
cant believe one day i will die

[related:]

how did that hole get there

if i tell people about the hole will they think it was me
who did it

[unrelated:]

take half-full cup of coffee place it under the hole
to collect spillage or at least give the illusion
of collecting spillage

[related:]

even if i could stomach breakfast i would never eat
weetabix

[unrelated:]

i will fix you tomorrow

[related:]

i will fix you tomorrow

how can i help you

when i cant even write a poem capable of saving the
world
when there are starving children suffering all over

can i serve you a coffee
can i serve you a hamburger
can i serve you a pint of best
can i serve you a degree

can i go to a seminar for advanced customer service
techniques
can i go to a job interview in a customer focused
environment

can i listen to the seminar leader + the interviewer tell
me
about company culture
about creating positive employee energy

can i cry honest tears
when they look at me
+ ask about my experiences
with great customer service

can i reveal my true passion
a passion for self-service machines
can i tell the seminar leader + the interviewer
that i use them all the time
that i think everyone should use them
that i envision a beautiful world
where all the starving children
have their very own self-service machines
+ that when these self-service machines say
unexpected item in bagging area
the starving children will look
in each of their bagging areas
+ the unexpected items will be happiness
+ they will all say *o look*   *its happiness*

will   the   seminar   leader   +   the   interviewer   then
ask me why it is that i love helping people so much

will i be able to reply that all i want
is to be paid to write poems in a 5* hotel
somewhere near the sea with an open bar

will the seminar leader + the interviewer then say
that im a good human being
that i can have lots of money
that they now respect me as a poet

will they give me my very own self-service machine
+ when i look in its bagging area
will i see that the world is a better place
will i be able to say to the world how can i help you
+ will the world smile back + say
dont worry – we are doing ok

i hope so

because if not
then i dont know how much longer
i can go on

thoughts on commute

fuck this world for stopping me from following my dreams

for instance right now i could be anything else - a sensor

feeling nothing but pure emotion - no thoughts no sense

of time - just a receptor for all the joy in the world i mean look at those lights those advertisement boards made by people doing what they love - i wonder if those models have to have shitty jobs on the side like me - i wonder if the people who hired them used to work retail - i mean imagine it - right now i could be experiencing nothing but all that innate happiness of the world - a world built by people who love what they do - untainted by thoughts of numbers - of hours - of pay - of bills - of time spent away from my writing - all this having to pretend - having to have zero feelings only thoughts about processes - having to be a machine doing one task repeatedly only worse than a machine

could do that task - you know if its true what the futurologists say - that machines will one day soon take our jobs - then i hope they hurry up because i am fed up right now of being contractually obliged to act like a

machine when all i want to be right now is nothing but a
sensor feeling nothing but pure emotion o look here i
am *hello how are you now pay me*

how to escape

the trap

this world is a trap
inside a man with a camera takes photos of me
over + over again
+ records everything i say

i dont say much
so its mostly silence
stabbed occasionally by my rumbling belly
or a groan of boredom
but its enough to shake me

enough to drive me out
to my car + i drive
+ i dont know where im going
+ all the roadsigns say *exit*
which i misread as *escape*
+ i follow them

+ the man with the camera follows me
or i think he does
he always seems to be there

+ the question now is not how do i get away from him
but how do i kill time before i get caught

so i reach into my bag as i drive
+ i find my filofax + i open it up + all the pages
are blank inside
+ all that white space all that messy chaotic
nothingness
looms over me like four magnolia walls
slowly surrounding me slanting forming a prison

+ i am still driving all around this world
looking for the perfect place to crash
some place with a view where i can leave my mark

until i end up at your place
+ you let me in with your humanity affirming smile
its like you know the world is on fire
but you just dont care
+ as i glance nervously out of each of your windows
you say *let him watch it doesnt matter anyway*

+ i know i cant stay here forever
i have things that i still dont know that i have to do
that i have to do
my filofax needs to be filled

the blank page walls painted all the colours + patterns
of the universe

but until then we just hold each other
+ i really dont do intimacy too well
but we still keep the curtains separate + the windows
wide open
+ wherever he is the man with the camera sits + waits
with only a lens for his eyes
while around him bright flames burst into hollow life
+ the flickering darkness of the entire world surrounds
him
in the most awesome most inescapable trap

things can only get better from here

i click on spam + hope
to get infected

as long as i keep praying
one of these days i know

ill wake up to find
my life greatly improved
by sunshine emoticons virtual pole dancers viagra pills
the coolest fonts hundreds of pounds from lost relatives
in africa five hundred pounds from a school friend stuck
in venezuela a thousand credits for roulette wheels ten
thousand tokens for live cam girls a hundred thousand
messages from russian singles in my local area a
million kisses from indian princesses who want to
marry me the greatest credit score the filthiest ladyboys
free dating accounts for all the fetish sites first access
to the best in amateur porn the newest online games
the biggest dick access to as many vibrators as needed
plastic surgery unlocked iphones unlimited ppi claims
cheap holidays to malaysia brand new glittery cursors
+ ill thank god
for these blessings

+ in return all i will give up

is my money my identity

my human form

+ ill embrace my ascent

^upwards to the aether^

==>where my self will spin through voids<==

$$$$b4 finAl1y DISAPERING$$$$

£££££int0 evryThing we EVER dReAmED£££££

<[]> <[]> <[]> about <[]> <[]> <[]>

whats the matter

the matter is
everything is shit
+ i am shit + so are you
+ all this shit matter
gets tangled up in all my shit poems
+ all my shit poems get tangled up
in all the shit mess of me

years ago i was sitting on a bus
thinking about the shitness of everything
at the stop before mine this kid got on
he couldnt stop smiling + i thought
that doesnt seem right
so i pushed past him
+ i got off that bus
+ i felt like shit
+ i didnt understand how

he couldnt understand how
everything is shit
but then maybe he did
maybe he secretly knew that everything is shit
+ maybe he knew that he was shit too
+ maybe he wrote shit poems

about all the shit matter that makes up his shit life

maybe he just smiled at all his shit matter
maybe he found the funniness in it all
maybe if i had stayed on that bus with him
it wouldve taken us both somewhere different
somewhere where everyone was free
to be completely shit together
somewhere where all the shit poems get published
in all the greatest shit literary journals

or maybe it wouldve just taken us somewhere shit

i guess it doesnt matter

because the matter is
that everything is shit
+ i am shit + so are you

but at least we sometimes get to get together
+ talk honestly about all our shit

be happy

read this poem [+ be happy]

answer your emails [+ be happy]

apply to some jobs [+ be happy]

eat breakfast [+ be happy]

drink decaffeinated herbal tea [+ be happy]

log into twitter [+ be happy]

go for a walk around the park [+ be happy]

watch ducks floating along [+ be happy]

buy some reduced price food [+ be happy]

delete your unused phone contacts [+ be happy]

think about your ex [+ be happy]

do yoga [+ be happy]

watch love island [+ be happy]

go to a poetry event [+ be happy]

watch a disney film [+ be happy]

lie [+ be happy]

text someone you havent talked to in ages [+ be happy]

cook instant noodles [+ be happy]

hold the hand of your significant other [+ be happy]

open your curtains [+ be happy]

click on random wikipedia hyperlinks [+ be happy]

write down your feelings [+ be happy]

go to a rope workshop at your local bdsm club [+ be happy]

think about what you want to eat later [+ be happy]

support your local immigrant communities [+ be happy]

go to church [+ be happy]

link me to all your socials [+ be happy]

eat five portions of fruit [+ be happy]

give up alcohol [+ be happy]

win a competition [+ be happy]

get published [+ be happy]

apply for creative scotland funding [+ be happy]

use plus signs in your poetry [+ be happy]

forgive those who have wronged you [+ be happy]

join scientology [+ be happy]

have more sex [+ be happy]

give up red meat [+ be happy]

get a salary job [+ be happy]

wash your face [+ be happy]

go to therapy [+ be happy]

research something you know nothing about [+ be happy]

go on a date [+ be happy]

have a baby [+ be happy]

drink water [+ be happy]

watch the football [+ be happy]

claim benefits [+ be happy]

go on holiday [+ be happy]

listen to lana del rey [+ be happy]

say no to racism [+ be happy]

ask me out [+ be happy]

jump on your bed like a kid again [+ be happy]

buy a pet [+ be happy]

have a conversation with someone you hate [+ be happy]

become celibate [+ be happy]

write to your local parliamentary representative [+ be happy]

make use of your local library [+ be happy]

plan a mad trip to france [+ be happy]

call your family more [+ be happy]

retweet positive messages from celebrities [+ be happy]

talk openly about your views on brexit [+ be happy]

kill all those who oppose you [+ be happy]

dance like nobody is watching [+ be happy]

purchase new ikea furniture [+ be happy]

hold onto me close [+ be happy]

please dont forget me [+ be happy]

be happy [+ be happy]

how to communicate

the blooming

if you believe old dead white male poets then the act of blooming
is a perfect metaphor for life - i mean after all *a young woman is like a flower in bloom*
which - according to some old dead white male scholar
-
is because the act of blooming is supposed to be some kind of
ecstatic moment of life - some time at which its finally possible
to both receive life + give life in equal measure - like how a flower
gives its pollen while receiving
sunshine or something

but if thats true then surely i am in bloom
since i am more than capable of giving + receiving
- especially giving fake smiles + receiving real money
ay my retail job

+ in fact my eyes must be in bloom
since they give me sight
while receiving light + colour + all that

+ my nose must be in bloom
since it gives me the ability to smell
while receiving smells in the first place

+ my hand must be in bloom
since it receives the things i grasp
+ gives back those things equally

+ actually my phone must be in bloom
since it receives tweets
+ gives me the ability to tweet back

+ this mirror must be in bloom
since it receives my image + gives my image
+ this lucky cat must be in bloom

+ this pen-pot must be in bloom

+ this plant must be in bloom
+ this chair must be in bloom
+ this window must be in bloom

+ this bin must be in bloom
+ this kitchen must be in bloom
+ this pan must be in bloom

+ this defrosting pack of reduced price
morrissons square sausage must be in bloom
+ this laptop must be in bloom too

+ the internet must be in bloom
+ this poem must be in bloom

except it isnt is it

just because everything gives + receives
doesnt mean its blooming

because giving + receiving isnt really some special
moment in life
its just what we do
its just what life is made of
its what life is

i mean it really is a shit metaphor

because a blooming flower eventually stops blooming
whereas we as people dont ever stop giving +
receiving

even if its just me giving my laptop some words
+ then receiving a way back to record those words

its still me proving my own life

which is a bit more beautiful than any flower i think
because life is beautiful
+ people are beautiful
+ my kitchen is beautiful
+ my phone is beautiful

whereas those old white male poets
they are not beautiful

they are not anything

because they are dead

closer

still thinking about the other night when i went
nonverbal

after talking with you successfully for a number of
hours

but it couldnt last – i didnt know what to say even
though

in my head our perfect conversation was still playing
out

with me still using my voice to transfer
the most perfect information pertinent to our status
as new-ish-ly formed friends testing that friendship to
see

if we could become better friends which is what i
wanted

since its hard to make close friends when you overthink
the nature of friendship too much instead of following
the internets advice + just acting natural
which if i understand correctly means talking
to people out loud about topics you know they are into
things like their other friends or interests or
relationships

you know – the other things in their lives they love

this is a qr code

follow me

this is a qr code
i made it online through a website which lets you
convert a url into a qr code [1]

to access it you need a
smart
phone or some other
device
on my phone its an app called optical reader

you then take a photo of the qr code
the app will then convert it back
to a url which can then be accessed on your phone

qr codes were invented in 1994 in japan
where they were used to help automotive companies
track the manufacture of different car parts
however with the rise in the number of people using
smartphones
these days qr codes can be found on everything from
bus stops to passports
advertising companies love them since they are both
non-invasive but also offer
an element of mystery - someone could say what could

this code lead to - or this one – or this one

if you were to scan the qr code from page 61 you will be led to the url of an instagram account i made [2]

upon which i have uploaded several photos of food i have eaten or cooked or bought

i did this since food is popular on instagram - its something we can all relate to

in 2008 a company in japan began selling tombstones featuring qr codes

scanning these codes would enable grievers to visit a virtual grave site of the deceased

wikipedia [3] says that in 2014 the jewish cemetery of la paz in uruguay began doing the same

wikipedia also says that qr codes can be used in currency or encryption but i prefer to stick to food

in 2016 i got my first instagram account i intended to try to become an instagram-poet [4] but

instead i spent all my time looking at food accounts – in a way it was like television

look at this meal look at that meal - a few months later i deleted it

the qr code on page 61 is the first qr code i have ever made

i was inspired by a poetry anthology i received which

featured them under different poems [5]

the codes they used would then link to audio or video
versions of the poems they were under
as if the publishers knew how intimidating a poem on a page
could be

i have definitely felt that – the intimidation of a poem – like
the intimidation of a meal
sometimes its not just the reading or the eating but the
thoughts of how or why it was made - scary

the letters q r in the phrase qr code stand for quick response
which makes no sense since to use them you have to first
own a smartphone

then open an app - then scan the code - then follow the link
whereas i could just write out a url which people could then
type instead
but then maybe that would be the same as writing out a
whole meal recipe
instead of just taking a photo of the finished product like
normal people do

i mean who cares really about the hows or the whys when
the end result looks so good

i was told the whole point of instagram is to gain followers
these followers will provide the account-holder with positive
reinforcement in their daily lives
while also making instagram as a business more profitable
which is another good thing

also if the account-holder is posting food photos then there
can be another positive
side if the cook or chef or restaurant is tagged as that can
create further marketing for them
one of the photos on my food instagram is of a box of roast
pork rice
i bought it for $4 from a shop in the manhattan chinatown
while visiting new york for the first time
i cant remember what it was called but it was some of the
best roast pork rice i have eaten
outside of hongkong – you should go there if you are ever in
the area
its on the street facing the southwestern corner of sara delano
roosevelt park

i could create a qr code to show you
but maybe the mystery is better
i could be lying - thats what people on instagram do

a qr code must include empty space around it – this is called a quiet zone [6]

this is similar to how bar codes used on food in supermarkets
require empty space
its important as it stops scanners from picking up interfering
information
that could stop the true purpose of the code from activating

i read on the internet that when bar codes were first
introduced some evangelical groups
believed they were the mark of the beast as prophesied by
certain biblical passages [7]
i havent heard the same being said about qr codes yet

qr codes are a new language like food is an old language
words are somewhere inbetween or around
occupying the quiet zones perhaps [8]

meanwhile i made my food instagram hours ago now
but still have zero followers
its not right i tell you

----
1 qr-code-generator.com
2 instagram.com/food2271412/
3 wikipedia.org
4 teenvogue.com/gallery/best-poets-on-instagram
5 badbettypress.com/product/the-dizziness-of-freedom/
6 qrworld.wordpress.com/2011/08/09/the-quiet-zone/
7 endtimestruth.com/666-2/barcode-technology-666
8 that may not be true but still it sounds good

the message

its never the same over skype + i know
that each time we talk could be the last
not for any dramatic reason like death
or illness simply because of time
zones + differences + our busy lives
which isnt to say that i blame time or
the world or even the internet for when
we do eventually fall out of communications
only that when it does happen i dont find it
easy + i still often think of you
make a plan to contact you + say hey
its been too long but then i dont + i guess
its because im scared that it will have been
too long or that you wont be ok anymore
+ that if you arent ok anymore that i wont be able
to help since im on the other side
of the world + the longer it gets the worse
i feel that i have already let you down
+ it becomes too easy to leave those feelings
alone + distract myself with immediate
surroundings immediate lives immediate
stresses + i guess its the same with you
but even if its not when you get this message
please just know that i do still think of you
+ i hope you are ok + that i am ok too

school prize

the year of the korea-japan world cup my school held
a raffle based around the competition + when i won
[i believe it was rigged so that every kid won
something] my prize was a pair of korea-japan world
cup branded chopsticks they were red plastic with the logo
up towards the top of each one where the calligraphy/detail
of a phoenix or dragon might normally go + they came
in their own special commemorative box + i felt
deflated due to the fact that i had wanted something better
[i cant remember what now] but my teacher
who i remember mostly as being kind + thoughtful
commented that at least someone won the chopsticks
who would use them
which i thought was a strange comment
since they were clearly japanese chopsticks + i am not
japanese so why would i use japanese chopsticks
especially when i had chinese chopsticks at home
which were bone-coloured plastic + had
cool phoenix + dragon details + calligraphy on them
but anyway i didnt say anything i just smiled + nodded
after all i was a winner + that is all
that really mattered

speculative books